How Is Honey Made?

by Grace Hansen

Abdo Kids Jumbo is an Imprint of Abdo Kids
abdobooks.com

abdobooks.com

Published by Abdo Kids, a division of ABDO, P.O. Box 398166, Minneapolis, Minnesota 55439.
Copyright © 2019 by Abdo Consulting Group, Inc. International copyrights reserved in all countries.
No part of this book may be reproduced in any form without written permission from the publisher.
Abdo Kids Jumbo™ is a trademark and logo of Abdo Kids.

102018

012019

 THIS BOOK CONTAINS
RECYCLED MATERIALS

Photo Credits: iStock, Shutterstock

Production Contributors: Teddy Borth, Jennie Forsberg, Grace Hansen

Design Contributors: Dorothy Toth, Laura Mitchell

Library of Congress Control Number: 2018945976

Publisher's Cataloging-in-Publication Data

Names: Hansen, Grace, author.

Title: How is honey made? / by Grace Hansen.

Description: Minneapolis, Minnesota : Abdo Kids, 2019 | Series: How is it made?
    Includes glossary, index and online resources (page 24).

Identifiers: ISBN 9781532181948 (lib. bdg.) | ISBN 9781532182921 (ebook) |
    ISBN 9781532183416 (Read-to-me ebook)

Subjects: LCSH: Honey--Juvenile literature. | Manufacturing processes--Juvenile
    literature. | Bee products industry--Juvenile literature.

Classification: DDC 641.38--dc23

Table of Contents

Sweet Honeybees 4

The Beekeeper 10

The Honey Factory 14

More Facts 22

Glossary 23

Index 24

Abdo Kids Code 24

Sweet Honeybees

Honeybees fly from flower
to flower collecting **nectar**.
They store the nectar in
their **pollen sacs**.

5

The bees fly back to the hive. Other bees suck the nectar out and chew it. This breaks the nectar down into simple sugars. The bees then place it in the honeycomb cells.

cell

Bees' flapping wings create heat. The heat helps the water in the sugars **evaporate**. Thick, sweet honey is left over. The bees cap the cells with wax.

9

The Beekeeper

The beekeeper sprays the hives with smoke. The smoke warns the bees.

The beekeeper puts a new cover on the hive. It smells like cherries. Bees do not like the smell. So they move toward the bottom of the hive.

The Honey Factory

The beekeeper removes each frame. The frames are brought to the honey factory. First, the wax is cut off of the frames.

14

frame

15

The frames are then put into a honey **extractor**. It spins to force the honey out of the cells.

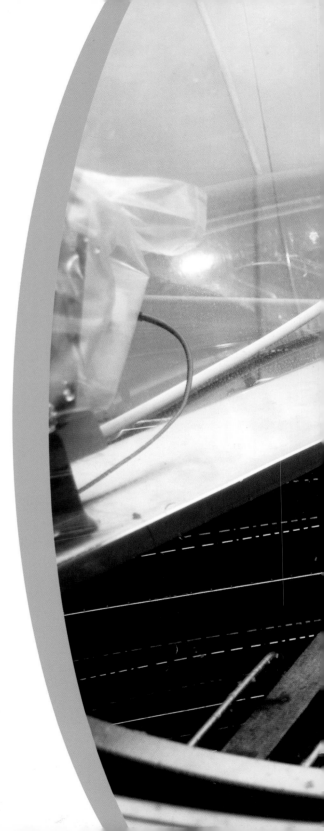

The honey is warmed to make it runnier. Then it is put through a strainer. This process takes out any remaining wax or **pollutants**.

The honey is ready to be bottled! Now it can be shipped!

More Facts

- One bee must fly about 55,000 miles (88,514 km) to make 1 pound (0.5 kg) of honey!

- A honeybee will visit 50 to 100 flowers in one trip to collect nectar.

- An average hive can make anywhere from 30 to 100 pounds (13.6 to 45.4 kg) of honey each year.

Glossary

evaporate – to turn from liquid into gas.

extractor – a machine that removes something using force.

nectar – the sweet liquid a plant makes that attracts insects.

pollen sac – one of the two sacs on a bee's hind leg that stores pollen and nectar.

pollutant – something that should not be there.

Index

beekeeper 10, 12, 14

bottling 20

cell 6, 8, 16

extractor 16

factory 14, 16, 18, 20

frame 14, 16

hive 6, 10, 12

honeybee 4, 6, 8, 10, 12

nectar 4, 6

strainer 18

Abdo Kids
ONLINE
FREE! ONLINE MULTIMEDIA RESOURCES

Visit **abdokids.com** and use this code to access crafts, games, videos, and more!

Abdo Kids Code:
HHK1948